THIS

MIGHTY

Book Belongs To

_____

DEAR MY

FELLOW GO-GETTERS, MOVERS & SHAKERS AND THE CURIOUSER & CURIOUSER!

I bid you welcome to the unparalleled guide for finding your ever-so-brilliant voice and engaging with the world.

This guide will push you to stand at the forefront, demand that you show up unwaveringly and dare you to remain undaunted in ways you never quite expected.

Don't delay! Take your guide and be a reporter of your own rare voice. Just be you, but do it brilliantly. Be unapologetic in your direction, add some swagger to your game, make some space for new conclusions, write all things down, create a little honest mayhem, find new ways of engaging with the world, and challenge every last thing you've been told.

Be mighty, you brilliant human, you daring crackerjack, you small and mighty! It's up to you now. I salute you.

Now, on your way!

ARE YOU...

(circle all that apply)

———

Mighty, Total Champ, Aces, Gutsy, Spontaneous, First-rate, Aboveboard, Well-meaning, Curiouser & Curiouser, Stalwart, Fighter, Hero-like, Headstrong, Well-informed, Daring, Foxy, Unorthodox, Rebellious, Plugged in, Matter-of-Fact, Neighborly, Forthright, Unbreakable, Saucy, Clever, A Mighty Spark, Happy-go-lucky, Frank, No-nonsense, Free & Easy, Noble-minded, Sharp, Fearless, Going for Broke, Plucky, Ungoverned, Hustling, Nonsensical, Reckless & Brave, With it, Smart-alecky, Crackerjack, Street Smart, Chin-up, Primo, Wild, Awe-inspiring, Loquacious, Psyched up, Rose-colored, Novel, Major-league, On Deck, Adventurous, Quick-witted, Cheeky, Footloose & Fancy-free, Sassy, Exuberant, Top Drawer, Self-possessed, Up to Snuff, Well-ordered, Collected, Magnanimous, Tough as Nails, Nonconformist, Shipshape, Audacious, Lionhearted, Razzle-dazzle, Imaginative, Whizkid, Undaunted, Gritty, Spirited, Gumptious, Up-and-Coming, Self-starting, Strident, On the Ball, Ballsy, Wide-awake, Nobody's Fool, Judicious, Big-hearted, Tops

(If you were even tempted to circle any of the above, we should get started!)

READY TO...

(circle all that apply)

———

Raise your voice, make waves,
break some rules, raise a little hell,
run wild, take to the streets, take a stand,
face the sky, never throw up your hands,
step on some toes, stand up to the bad guys,
right a few wrongs, dare to do everything,
make some racket, face down wrongdoing,
run amok, get out of line, stand out,
turn the tables on end, make a fuss,
champion change, rise up, resist small-
mindedness, dare to be gutsy, be one of
the good ones, outbrave the brave,
outrage the riffraff, call their bluff?

Ready, Set, Go!

PLEDGE

I do solemnly pledge

that I will, with all the mightiness I can muster, take charge of my awesome life. I will do so wholly, earnestly and altogether brilliantly.

I will try to be matchless in my convictions, my curiosity, my heroism and my unwavering fearlessness.

I will do my best, come hell or high water, to raise my voice for all the right things, to right as many wrongs as are put in my path, to take a stand for the underdogs and the less mighty, to give no ifs, ands or buts, to raise a little hell with thoughtful purpose, to be mindful with my gratitude, to demand all that I deserve and to unwaveringly endeavor to be awesome, rebellious, heroic, fearless, curious, gutsy, frank, unbreakable, daring, spontaneous, forthright, sharp, wild, awe-inspiring, self-possessed, audacious, undaunted, a little gritty, strident, no-nonsense, saucy, brilliant, well-informed, wide awake and Small & Mighty!

And, above all, I will fight for, defend, back, ride shotgun for and cheer on mighty humans in ALL of life's awesome pursuits.

Congrats. Welcome to the club.

LAW & ORDER

(aka: all the rules)

Here are some important safety tips, rules, regulations, rights, duties and obligations to adhere to while employing your Small & Mighty Guidebook (please pick and choose at random):

Participate! Rock the boat. Take up space. Show up. Be excellent. Use your wit. Be unapologetically yourself. Draw outside the lines. Don't fit in. Call BS on a majority and ignore most others. Don't believe in impossible. Make your very own rules. Volunteer. Join in the protest. Lend a hand. Be anything but "normal!" Pretend to be brave—even if for a brief time. Find your way in the world. Play 'til the cows come home. Speak up. Challenge the norms. Make a right mess of things. Sit in. Do the opposite. Consider all things an experiment. Know who you are. Lead the mutiny. Don't even try to fit in. Keep your chin up. Offer your kindness. Seek out the absurd. Be willing to say, "I just don't know." Take chances. Be loud about your existence. Shout out. Shake things up. Step into the unknown. Be all in. Risk everything (including making a fool of yourself). Use your imagination to its depths. Vote. Bend the rules. Make mistakes (many, many mistakes). Start from scratch. Radically transform whatever moment you are in. Play the devil's advocate. Avoid authority. Try never to be a naysayer. See the good. Leave your ego at the door. Live by your own set of rules. Know that ALL things are possible. Carpe diem! Always remain open to the magic of it all and, for the sake of all that is holy, question everything! Oh, and if all else fails and the rules just don't work in your favor, break them and don't look back!

Inhale. Exhale. Begin.

MY
Mighty
MANIFESTO

I, _____ (Name or Reporter Name),
pledge these _____ (s) to be
downright unquestionable. This is my
_____ and my
_____ and I shall move ahead
with _____ . I am filled with guts
and will at no time _____ .
I _____ by my own rules and will,
without excuses, _____ . I will use
my _____ for only awesome things and
be _____ in the process. I plan to be
the mighty in my own _____ and be
_____ at finding my voice in
the world.

I am Small & Mighty!

FULL NAME:

REPORTER NAME:

NAME I'D RATHER HAVE:

Date Of Birth:

Hair Color:

Height:

Eye Color:

EMERGENCY CONTACT:
(for rare cases of enthusiastic rebellion, unaccounted for twists and turns and occasional chaos!)

Outgoingness:

1   2   3   4   5   6   7   8   9   10
(Introvert)   (Extrovert)

Star Sign:

FAVORITE MIGHTY QUOTE:

ONE TRUE GOAL IN LIFE:

_____

_____

_____

_____

_____

3 UNCHALLENGED FEARS:

_____

_____

_____

OTHER NOTES:

_____

_____

_____

_____

_____

_____

_____

Table OF CONTENTS

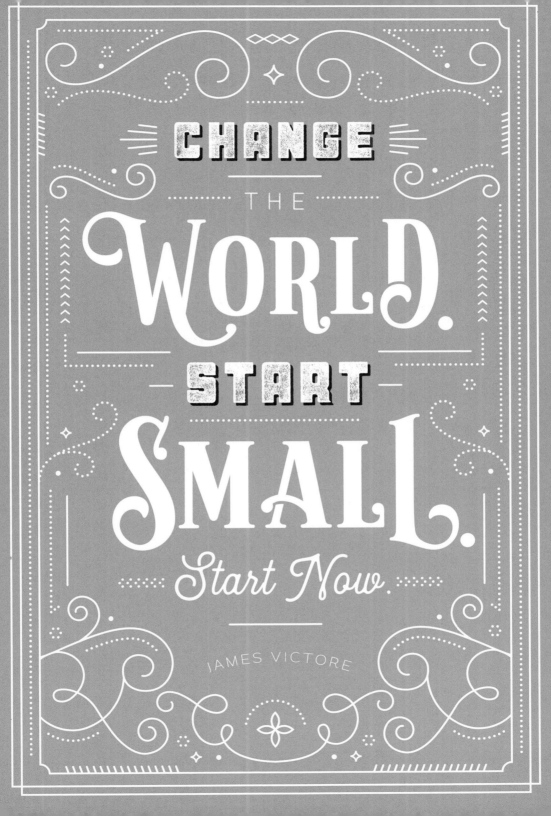

CHAPTER ONE

MIGHTY
REBEL

MIGHTY
REBEL

·················

THIS CHAPTER CHAMPIONS

every mighty rebel, all the stalwart
renegades, any daring protester and
every brand of mover and shaker.
Find your voice here by using it like a
powerhouse, discovering the confidence
in your own opinions, figuring out what
makes you tick, and, with conviction,
deciding how your greatness can
change the world.

Alright,

READY, SET, GO!

MAKE NO MISTAKE I AM FIERCE.

—NANEA HOFFMAN

Two outspoken activists?

_____

_____

What makes them so decidedly outspoken?

_____

_____

_____

Two mighty rebels?

_____

_____

What makes them so decidedly mighty?

_____

_____

_____

Two momentous leaders?

_____

_____

What makes them so decidedly momentous?

_____

_____

_____

Two gutsy revolutionaries?

_____

_____

What makes them so decidedly gutsy?

_____

_____

_____

Two fiery public speakers?

_____

_____

What makes them so decidedly fiery?

_____

_____

_____

Write, record, ruminate, chew over, cogitate and ponder *all* your burning questions about rebellion, uprising and spirited defiance. What would you ask if you could ask absolutely anything?

Do one thing every day
THAT IS
REBELLIOUS

_____   _____

_____   _____

_____   _____

_____   _____

_____   _____

_____   _____

_____   _____

_____   _____

_____   _____

_____   _____

_____   _____

QUESTION *Everything*

What makes a rebel a rebel?

_____

_____

_____

What rules don't make sense to you?

_____

_____

_____

What is the wildest thing you've ever done?

_____

_____

_____

What isn't fair?

_____

_____

_____

What wild thing would you like to do but haven't?

_____

_____

_____

Is something stopping you from doing what you want?

_____

_____

_____

100 REBELLIOUS

Sketches

Take these two pages and pencil in, scribble about, trace and sketch the first 100 rebellious things you think of. The sheer number gets you through the obvious and on to the good stuff. Let's see what you uncover!

YOU
HAVE TO ACT
— AS IF IT'S POSSIBLE —
TO RADICALLY TRANSFORM THE
WORLD
— & YOU HAVE TO DO THAT —
All The Time.

ANGELA DAVIS

Renegade SCAVENGER

· · · · · · · · · · · · · · · · · · · ·

Set out on a scavenger hunt!
Take pictures, collect things
& size up your findings!

☐ A PHOTO OF YOU IN FRONT OF YOUR
LOCAL POLICE PRECINCT
Date: Location:
Description: _____
_____
_____

☐ A PODIUM
Date: Location:
Description: _____
_____
_____

☐ A POLITICAL CAMPAIGN SIGN
Date: Location:
Description: _____
_____
_____

☐ POLITICAL GRAFFITI
Date: Location:
Description: _____
_____
_____

☐ THE NAME OF YOUR CITY, TOWN
OR NEIGHBORHOOD
Date: Location:
Description: _____
_____
_____

☐ A FLAG OF YOUR COUNTRY
Date: Location:
Description: _____
_____
_____

☐ A REBELLIOUS BUMPER STICKER
Date: Location:
Description: _____
_____
_____

☐ A FLYER FOR A MARCH, RALLY
OR PROTEST
Date: Location:
Description: _____
_____
_____

☐ A POWERFUL QUOTE PUBLICLY DISPLAYED
Date: Location:
Description: _____
_____
_____

☐ A SYMBOL REPRESENTING ANY
POLITICAL MARCH
Date: Location:
Description: _____
_____
_____

Notes:
_____
_____
_____

○ Volunteer to help in a political campaign

○ Attend a protest

○ Write a new set of rules you wish your local leaders would implement

○ Create a series of unruly march slogan posters

○ Write down ALL of your own political views

○ Find a venue to give a public speech

○ Identify rallies or marches happening in your area

○ Sport a sticker that's somewhat controversial

○ Attend a meeting in your own town hall or community center

○ Create your own rebel postcards & mail them to people in power

○ Identify outdated and absurd laws in your state or region

○ Write letters of encouragement to your favorite public officials

○ Do 30 rebellious things in 30 days

○ March in a rally

○ Chat with one new person every day for a week about something controversial

○ Write an interview you'd like to give to someone famous

○ Write the speech you would give if you were the president

○ Write 100 changes you would like to see happen in the world

○ Create a personal campaign poster

NOTES:

_____

_____

_____

_____

WORDS Have POWER

Create an ongoing list of the raddest words, sayings and ideas
for rally posters and march signs. Write them down here!

_____   _____
_____   _____
_____   _____

_____   _____
_____   _____
_____   _____

_____   _____
_____   _____
_____   _____

_____   _____
_____   _____
_____   _____

_____   _____
_____   _____
_____   _____

_____   _____
_____   _____
_____   _____

BE A JOURNALIST

Be a journalist, a writer, a reporter and a storyteller!
Go out into your community, area and around your familiar
stomping grounds and start asking other humans bold and
interesting questions about how they are mighty rebels and
renegades in the world.

ASK 10 QUESTIONS:
(Be gutsy and bold with who you chat with. Ask the hard stuff. Ask it all.)

_____

_____

_____

_____

_____

_____

_____

_____

_____

_____

_____

_____

_____

_____

_____

_____

_____

_____

NOTICE EVERY DETAIL:
(This is where you'll likely hear the *real* story, the good stuff and the whole truth.)

_____

_____

_____

_____

_____

_____

_____

_____

_____

_____

_____

_____

_____

_____

_____

_____

_____

_____

_____

_____

_____

_____

_____

Now, after you've collected your thoughts, their thoughts, all the brilliant
details and all points of view and notions, evaluate, digest and try to sum
up the new knowledge into your own mighty format (as a soap box orator,
a slam poet, a singer/songwriter or a political character).
Use your voice to report the findings.

WRITER'S REVIVAL

Bring back letter writing! Write a letter, a pile of postcards or tons of lengthy correspondences to **elected officials about a cause you believe in**. Ask questions, be curious, be bold, be genuine, be real, be interested. Write right now!

LETTER TO:

_____

QUESTIONS TO ASK:

_____
_____
_____

LETTER TO:

_____

QUESTIONS TO ASK:

_____
_____
_____

LETTER TO:

_____

QUESTIONS TO ASK:

_____
_____
_____

SKETCH *your* OWN

Sketch, plan, devise, hatch, plot, brainstorm & create some of your very own rebel march and rally poster ideas! Be fearless with your words and brazen with your execution. Send your messages out into the world!

Oh, ALL THE RULES I'LL CHANGE!

Dig into the more meaningful things, every manner of significance, and, most especially, your far-reaching future. Dig up and record all of the crazy rules that are out there that you'd like to change. I'm guessing you'll surprise yourself with one mighty list!

Write The Rules

Here's your chance to write your own rules, new rules, never-discussed rules, outdated rules, broken rules, rules that are off limits, time-honored rules, unwritten rules, old rules, family rules, rarely followed rules, simple rules and even unspoken rules. Stamp them in ink, sign on the dotted line—this is your awesome life now.

1 _____

2 _____

3 _____

4 _____

5 _____

6 _____

7 _____

8 _____

9 _____

10 _____

11 _____

12 _____

13 _____

14 _____

15 _____

Would you RATHER?

(circle your answers)

HAVE TO SAY WHATEVER COMES TO MIND IMMEDIATELY *or* NEVER BE ABLE
TO SPEAK AGAIN?

BE ABLE TO CHANGE THE PAST *or* SEE THE FUTURE?

LIVE IN A UTOPIA AS A NORMAL PERSON *or* IN A DYSTOPIA AS THE SUPREME RULER?

KNOW THE UNCOMFORTABLE TRUTH OF THE WORLD *or* BELIEVE A COMFORTING LIE?

BE ABLE TO DETECT ANY LIE YOU HEAR *or* GET AWAY WITH ANY LIE YOU TELL?

CREATE HISTORY *or* CHANGE IT?

BECOME FAMOUS *or* POWERFUL?

BE ABLE TO DODGE ANYTHING DANGEROUS *or* BE ABLE TO ASK ANY 3 QUESTIONS
AND HAVE THEM ANSWERED?

SUDDENLY BE ELECTED A SENATOR *or* BECOME A CEO OF A MAJOR COMPANY?

BE FAMOUS BUT RIDICULED *or* BE JUST A NORMAL PERSON?

BE COMPLETELY INVISIBLE FOR ONE DAY *or* BE ABLE TO FLY FOR ONE DAY?

BE ALONE FOR THE REST OF YOUR LIFE *or* ALWAYS BE SURROUNDED
BY ANNOYING PEOPLE?

BE INFAMOUS IN HISTORY BOOKS *or* BE FORGOTTEN AFTER YOUR DEATH?

HAVE A HORRIBLY CORRUPT GOVERNMENT *or* HAVE NO GOVERNMENT AT ALL?

BELIEVING GAME

Get a group of friends together and pick a controversial issue that you believe strongly in. Now, ask everyone to suspend all judgment and consider seriously another viewpoint. Open yourselves up to and work at believing some parts to the other side of the story.

1. Introduce the controversial issue or topic to the group:

_____

_____

_____

_____

_____

_____

2. Have everyone write down their initial thinking on the issue:

_____

_____

_____

_____

_____

_____

3. Now, ask everyone to read what they wrote out loud.

4. Conduct a small group discussion allowing participants to ONLY make statements that agree with one point of view. Do not make any negative or even challenging statements.

5. Finally, discuss together the experiences everyone had while they were asked to suspend their judgments and consider the other side of the argument. What felt right? Did they feel like something changed inside at all? Did the experience feel authentic? How did they perceive others' arguments on the issue? Did anything affect their points of view even slightly?

WHAT'S *Your* STORY?

Write down your **REBEL STORY**—your point of view on what it feels like when you're a rebel and a renegade and a mover & shaker.

Write all of your thoughts and theories and feelings about what makes you a mighty first-rate rebel.

_____

_____

_____

_____

_____

_____

_____

_____

_____

_____

_____

_____

_____

_____

_____

_____

_____

_____

_____

_____

_____

_____

_____

As you travel through the world, you're bound to have brilliant realizations, crazy insights and sudden inspiration—if you're open to them. Here's where you can write these things down.

Record your aha moments and determine how they will help you continue moving, only forward!

Mighty BADGES

ALMIGHTY

GUTSY

MIGHTY
**UN
STOP
PABLE**

FEARLESS
LEADER
SOCIETY

Mighty
RENEGADE

Mighty
REBEL

Mover AND
SHAKER

CHAPTER TWO

· · · · · · · · · · · ·

MIGHTY

HERO

MIGHTY
HERO

·················

THIS CHAPTER CHAMPIONS
every mighty hero, all magnanimous
do-gooders, any community patron,
and every sort of well-meaning champion.
Find your voice here by searching for
any and all ways to give back, doing all
things far-reaching in the community,
being a strong example of the
big-hearted and discovering your
own superhero-ness in the world.

Now,
BRING IT!

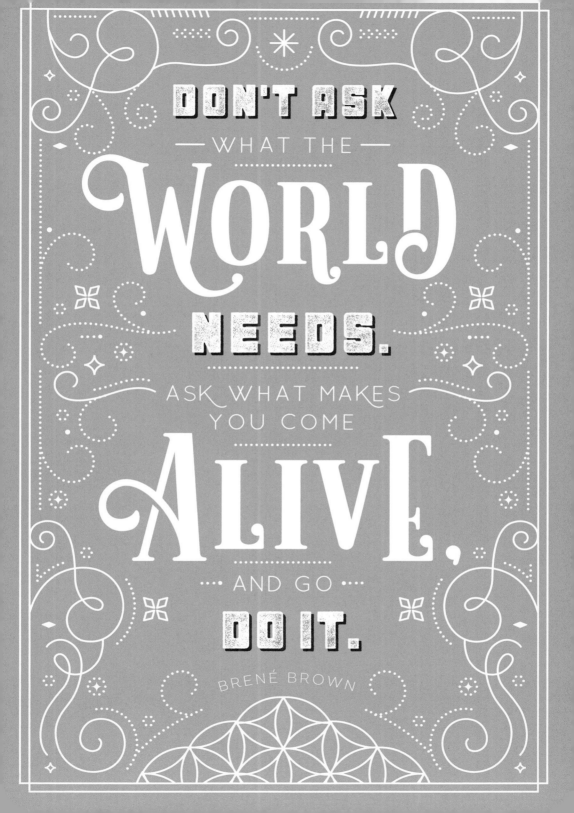

DON'T ASK
— WHAT THE —
WORLD
NEEDS.
ASK WHAT MAKES
YOU COME
ALIVE,
··· AND GO ···
DO IT.
BRENÉ BROWN

Can you **NAME:**

Two notable Nobel Prize winners?

_____

_____

What makes them so decidedly noteworthy?

_____

_____

_____

Two rare heroes?

_____

_____

What makes them so decidedly rare?

_____

_____

_____

Two noble humanitarians?

_____

_____

What makes them so decidedly noble?

_____

_____

_____

Two world-class volunteers?

_____

_____

What makes them so decidedly world class?

_____

_____

_____

Two uncommon philanthropists?

_____

_____

What makes them so decidedly uncommon?

_____

_____

_____

QUESTIONS

Write, record, ruminate, chew over, cogitate and ponder *all* your burning questions about philanthropy, social conscience and plain ol' superhero ways. What would you ask if you could ask absolutely anything?

Do one thing every day
THAT IS
HEROIC

_____

_____

_____

_____

_____

_____

_____

_____

_____

_____

QUESTION *Everything*

What makes a hero a hero?

_____

_____

_____

What superhero power do you wish you had?

_____

_____

_____

If you could be invisible for one day, what would you do?

_____

_____

_____

What one thing makes you feel the most brave?

_____

_____

_____

Who do you wish you were?

_____

_____

_____

What are you most proud of?

_____

_____

_____

100 HEROIC Sketches

Take these two pages and pencil in, scribble about, trace and sketch the first 100 heroic things you think of. The sheer number gets you through the obvious and on to the good stuff. Let's see what you uncover!

Don't stop now, keep sketching!

DO NOT
THINK LESS
of
YOURSELF
IF YOU CAN'T
be
FEARLESS.
DOING IT AFRAID
IS JUST AS
BRAVE.

MORGAN HARPER NICHOLS

Superhero
SCAVENGER

· · · · · · · · · · · · · · · · · · ·

Set out on a scavenger hunt!
Take pictures, collect things
& size up your findings!

☐ **A NONPROFIT BUSINESS**
Date: Location:
Description: _____
_____
_____

☐ **A CAPE**
Date: Location:
Description: _____
_____
_____

☐ **THE WORD "KINDNESS" PUBLICLY DISPLAYED**
Date: Location:
Description: _____
_____
_____

☐ **A TROPHY**
Date: Location:
Description: _____
_____
_____

☐ **A PHOTO OF YOU IN FRONT OF A COMMUNITY CENTER**
Date: Location:
Description: _____
_____
_____

☐ **YOUR REFLECTION**
Date: Location:
Description: _____
_____
_____

☐ **A FLYER LOOKING FOR VOLUNTEERS**
Date: Location:
Description: _____
_____
_____

☐ **A GOLD STAR**
Date: Location:
Description: _____
_____
_____

☐ **A THUMBS UP!**
Date: Location:
Description: _____
_____
_____

☐ **A SUPERHERO ACTION FIGURE**
Date: Location:
Description: _____
_____
_____

Notes:
_____
_____
_____

- ○ Wear a superhero cape every day for a week
- ○ Do something heroic for someone for the next 30 days
- ○ Volunteer at a community suicide prevention event
- ○ Help 10 people today
- ○ Create your own superhero character
- ○ Give everyone you see today a thumbs up!
- ○ Take your neighbor a meal or treat for an entire week
- ○ Donate your time to a local nonprofit
- ○ Write your own superhero story
- ○ Visit someone who lives alone
- ○ Write a list of 30 ways someone like you can give back to their community
- ○ Write a handwritten letter to your own personal superhero
- ○ Take part in a disaster clean-up crew
- ○ Write down your top 30 wishes
- ○ Volunteer your time at a community center
- ○ Research what it means to be a humanitarian
- ○ Identify your favorite 6 Nobel Prize winners
- ○ Create flyers for organizations needing volunteers
- ○ Help someone move into their new home
- ○ Walk around your town handing out gold stars

NOTES:

_____

_____

_____

_____

DRAW *Your* OWN

Draw, play, scheme and plot your very own superhero cape ideas.
Use your skills, your unquestionable spirit and brilliant heart to come up
with something magical!

BE A JOURNALIST

Be a journalist, a writer, a reporter and a storyteller!
Go out into your community, area and around your familiar
stomping grounds and start asking other humans bold and
interesting questions about how they are mighty heroes and
do-gooders in the world.

ASK 10 QUESTIONS:

(Be gutsy and bold with who you chat with. Ask the hard stuff. Ask it all.)

_____

_____

_____

_____

_____

_____

_____

_____

_____

_____

_____

_____

_____

_____

_____

_____

_____

_____

_____

_____

NOTICE EVERY DETAIL:

(This is where you'll likely hear the *real* story, the good stuff and the whole truth.)

_____

_____

_____

_____

_____

_____

_____

_____

_____

_____

_____

_____

_____

_____

_____

_____

_____

_____

_____

_____

_____

_____

_____

_____

_____

Now, after you've collected your thoughts, their thoughts, all the brilliant
details and all points of view and notions, evaluate, digest and try to sum
up the new knowledge into your own mighty format (as a soap box orator,
a slam poet, a singer/songwriter or a political character).
Use your voice to report the findings.

RANDOM ACTS OF

Kindness

What amazing things have you done that no one was around to see?

WRITER'S REVIVAL

Bring back letter writing! Write a letter, a pile of postcards or tons of lengthy correspondences to **your biggest heroes making a difference in the world**. Ask questions, be curious, be bold, be genuine, be real, be interested. Write right now!

LETTER TO:

_____

QUESTIONS TO ASK:

_____

_____

_____

LETTER TO:

_____

QUESTIONS TO ASK:

_____

_____

_____

LETTER TO:

_____

QUESTIONS TO ASK:

_____

_____

_____

SITUATIONAL HERO

Identify, observe and then plan a way to help solve a current issue
or community problem that you're fiercely fired up about.

Situation:

_____

_____

_____

How will you try and "fix" it?

_____

_____

_____

_____

_____

_____

_____

_____

_____

_____

_____

_____

_____

_____

this I BELIEVE

Sum up what you believe on one page. Maybe it's about doing good or being curious or becoming a superhero, but whatever it is, you can bet that it's important. Do it now; write it all down!

Would you RATHER?

(circle your answers)

SAVE THE LIFE OF SOMEONE YOU'RE CLOSE TO *or* SAVE THE LIVES OF FIVE RANDOM STRANGERS?

EXPERIENCE A PERPETUAL WATER BALLOON WAR GOING ON IN YOUR CITY/TOWN *or* A PERPETUAL FOOD FIGHT?

BE ABLE TO TELEPORT ANYWHERE *or* BE ABLE TO READ MINDS?

BE ABLE TO SEE 10 MINUTES INTO YOUR OWN FUTURE *or* 10 MINUTES INTO THE FUTURE OF ANYONE BUT YOURSELF?

BE AN UNIMPORTANT CHARACTER IN THE LAST MOVIE YOU SAW *or* IN THE LAST BOOK YOU READ?

BE COMPELLED TO HIGH FIVE EVERYONE YOU MEET *or* RANDOMLY HUG ANYONE YOU SEE WEARING A GREEN SHIRT?

BE ABLE TO CONTROL FIRE *or* WATER?

HAVE SUPER-SENSITIVE TASTE *or* SUPER-SENSITIVE HEARING?

HELD IN HIGH REGARD BY YOUR PARENTS *or* YOUR FRIENDS?

BECOME FAMOUS *or* BECOME POWERFUL?

HAVE HANDS THAT KEPT GROWING AS YOU GOT OLDER *or* HAVE FEET THAT KEPT GROWING AS YOU GOT OLDER?

DONATE YOUR BODY TO SCIENCE *or* DONATE YOUR ORGANS TO A PERSON WHO NEEDS THEM?

Oh, ALL THE GOOD I'LL DO!

Dig into the more meaningful things, every manner of significance, and, most especially, your far-reaching future. Look into and record all of the good things you'd like to add to the world. I'm guessing you'll surprise yourself with one mighty list!

_____   _____

_____   _____

_____   _____

_____   _____

_____   _____

_____   _____

_____   _____

_____   _____

_____   _____

_____   _____

_____   _____

_____   _____

WHAT'S *Your* STORY?

Write down your **HERO STORY**—your point of view on what it feels like when you're a hero and a do-gooder and a well-meaning champion.

Write all of your thoughts and theories and feelings about what makes you a mighty first-rate hero.

_____

_____

_____

_____

_____

_____

_____

_____

_____

_____

_____

_____

_____

_____

_____

_____

_____

_____

As you travel through the world, you're bound to have brilliant realizations, crazy insights and sudden inspiration—if you're open to them. Here's where you can write these things down.

Record your aha moments and determine how they will help you continue moving, only forward!

Mighty BADGES

YOU'VE EARNED YOUR STRIPES

· LEGENDARY ·

MIGHTY
HERO

FIREBALL

Crushing
IT

Gold
STAR

Superhero
CAPE
CLUB

Mighty
— LIGHTNING —
ROD

CHAPTER THREE

....

MIGHTY

NOMAD

MIGHTY
NOMAD

. . . .

THIS CHAPTER CHAMPIONS

every self-possessed adventurer,
any unorthodox wanderer, all global
explorers and every variety of curious
traveler. Find your voice here by generating
an interest in your world, roving across
cultural ideas, moving around in your
arena and being a mighty representative
of all things afoot.

Okay,

GO GET 'EM, TIGER!

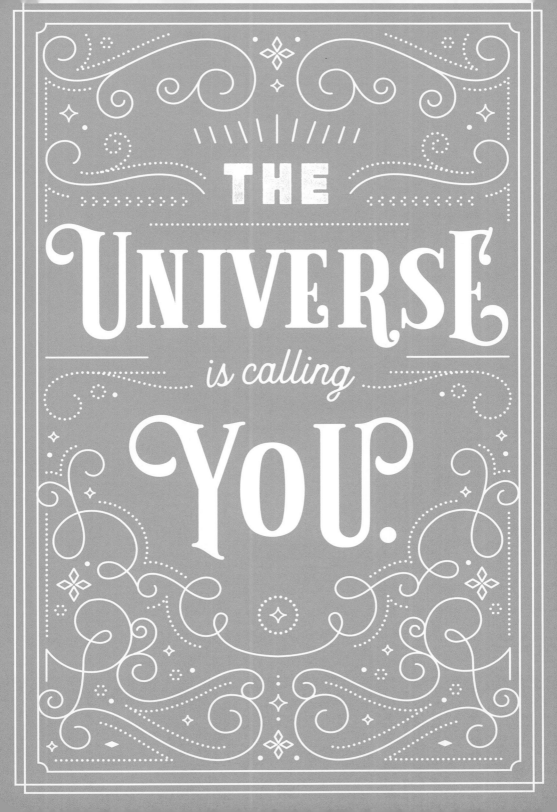

Two world-famous travelers?

_____

_____

What makes them so decidedly world famous?

_____

_____

_____

Two unordinary adventurers?

_____

_____

What makes them so decidedly unordinary?

_____

_____

_____

Two daring pioneers?

_____

_____

What makes them so decidedly daring?

_____

_____

_____

Two gritty journalists?

_____

_____

What makes them so decidedly gritty?

_____

_____

_____

Two hot-shot ambassadors?

_____

_____

What makes them so decidedly hot shot?

_____

_____

_____

QUESTIONS

Write, record, ruminate, chew over, cogitate and ponder *all* your burning questions about things that matter globally, cultural curiosities and unorthodox traveling. What would you ask if you could ask absolutely anything?

Do one thing every day
THAT IS
ADVENTUROUS

_____

_____

_____

_____

_____

_____

_____

_____

_____

QUESTION *Everything*

What makes a traveler a traveler?

_____

_____

_____

Where would you live if you could live anywhere?

_____

_____

_____

What would the perfect secret hideout look like?

_____

_____

_____

What things are currently in your bag?

_____

_____

_____

Where would you go to have an epic adventure?

_____

_____

_____

What is the very best thing in the world?

_____

_____

_____

100 ADVENTUROUS

Sketches

Take these two pages and pencil in, scribble about, trace and sketch the first 100 adventurous things you think of. The sheer number gets you through the obvious and on to the good stuff. Let's see what you uncover!

Don't stop now, keep sketching!

ONE

LIFE.

JUST ONE.

WHY AREN'T WE

RUNNING

LIKE WE ARE ON FIRE

TOWARD

our wildest

DREAMS?

Adventure SCAVENGER

• • • • • • • • • • • • • • • • • •

Set out on a scavenger hunt!
Take pictures, collect things
& size up your findings!

☐ SOMETHING IN A FOREIGN LANGUAGE

Date: Location:

Description:
_____
_____
_____

☐ A TRAIL MARKER

Date: Location:

Description:
_____
_____
_____

☐ A RELAXING PLACE

Date: Location:

Description:
_____
_____
_____

☐ A PASSPORT PHOTO BOOTH

Date: Location:

Description:
_____
_____
_____

☐ THE PERFECT TRAVEL KIT

Date: Location:

Description:
_____
_____
_____

☐ AN OLD ROAD MAP

Date: Location:

Description:
_____
_____
_____

☐ A FOREIGN NEWSPAPER

Date: Location:

Description:
_____
_____
_____

☐ A BRILLIANT JOURNEY QUOTE

Date: Location:

Description:
_____
_____
_____

☐ AN AIRPLANE ICON

Date: Location:

Description:
_____
_____
_____

☐ AN ETHNIC FOOD MARKET

Date: Location:

Description:
_____
_____
_____

Notes:
_____
_____
_____

○ Create a dream travel list

○ Visit a popular local tourist destination

○ Identify crazy (to you) laws from other countries

○ Start learning a foreign language for a country you want to visit

○ Plan an overseas trip itinerary

○ Get to know all of the important cultural customs of your dream place to travel to

○ Research the idea of voluntourism

○ Volunteer with a global nonprofit

○ Try 30 adventurous things for the next 30 days

○ Try one foreign treat every day this week

○ Start a list of everything you wish to try if you could only choose one place to visit

○ Start a friendship with a foreign pen pal

○ Help out a community green clean-up crew

○ Research areas of current conflict in the world

○ Take a hike you've never thought to take before

○ Identify which countries require visas and which require only passports to travel to

○ Plan a globally themed dinner party for friends

○ Identify each and every airport in your state or region

○ Draw your own dream map of the world

○ Get (or update) your travel passport

NOTES:

_____

_____

_____

PLOT *Your* OWN

Plot, contrive, scribble and jot down your very own adventurer T-shirt ideas. Be bold with your ideas, gutsy with your words and loud with your colors to say something with moxie!

BE A JOURNALIST

Be a journalist, a writer, a reporter and a storyteller!
Go out into your community, area and around your familiar
stomping grounds and start asking other humans bold and
interesting questions about how they are mighty adventurers
and travelers in the world.

ASK 10 QUESTIONS:
(Be gutsy and bold with who you chat with. Ask the hard stuff. Ask it all.)

NOTICE EVERY DETAIL:
(This is where you'll likely hear the *real* story, the good stuff and the whole truth.)

_____
_____
_____
_____
_____
_____
_____
_____
_____
_____
_____
_____
_____
_____
_____
_____
_____
_____
_____
_____
_____
_____
_____
_____

Now, after you've collected your thoughts, their thoughts, all the brilliant
details and all points of view and notions, evaluate, digest and try to sum
up the new knowledge into your own mighty format (as a soap box orator,
a slam poet, a singer/songwriter or a political character).
Use your voice to report the findings.

- ○ Gotten lost
- ○ Hailed a taxi
- ○ Flown in a helicopter
- ○ Strayed from the beaten path
- ○ Planned a trip
- ○ Taken an overnight train
- ○ Ridden in a speed boat
- ○ Hiked a steep mountain
- ○ Climbed a tree
- ○ Eaten an insect
- ○ Written an itinerary
- ○ Broken the rules
- ○ Taken a detour
- ○ Traveled to a foreign country
- ○ Followed a paper map

- ○ Had a picnic in a field
- ○ Entered through the exit door
- ○ Hiked without shoes
- ○ Gone skydiving
- ○ Eaten a progressive dinner
- ○ Used the shortcut
- ○ Walked around with your eyes closed
- ○ Gone where the wind blew you
- ○ Used chopsticks
- ○ Driven fast on a dirt road
- ○ Been seasick
- ○ Skipped around town
- ○ Met a queen
- ○ Picked up litter
- ○ Bicycled in another city

Give yourself points if you want to: _____

WRITER'S REVIVAL

Bring back letter writing! Write a letter, a pile of postcards or tons of lengthy correspondences to **famed adventurers that have braved daring feats**. Ask questions, be curious, be bold, be genuine, be real, be interested. Write right now!

LETTER TO:

_____

QUESTIONS TO ASK:

_____

_____

_____

LETTER TO:

_____

QUESTIONS TO ASK:

_____

_____

_____

LETTER TO:

_____

QUESTIONS TO ASK:

_____

_____

_____

Draw Adventure Details

Someting Heroic ···

DATE: _____ LOCATION: _____

Someting Heroic ···

DATE: _____ LOCATION: _____

Someting Heroic ••

DATE: _____ LOCATION: _____

Someting Heroic ••

DATE: _____ LOCATION: _____

Someting Heroic ••

DATE: _____ LOCATION: _____

Oh, ALL THE PLACES I'LL GO!

Dig into the more meaningful things, every manner of significance, and, most especially, your far-reaching future. Research and record all of the crazy places you'd like to go. I'm guessing you'll surprise yourself with one mighty list!

Would you RATHER?

(circle your answers)

BE AN AMAZING DANCER *or* BE AN AMAZING SINGER?

LIVE IN THE COUNTRY *or* LIVE IN THE CITY?

SEE THE WORLD BUT LIVE IN POVERTY *or* STAY IN ONE PLACE AND LIVE RICH?

BE COVERED IN FUR *or* BE COVERED IN SCALES?

BE ABLE TO TALK TO LAND ANIMALS, ANIMALS THAT FLY, *or* ANIMALS THAT LIVE UNDERWATER?

TRAVEL THE WORLD FOR A YEAR ON A SHOESTRING BUDGET *or* STAY IN ONLY ONE COUNTRY FOR A YEAR BUT LIVE FIRST-CLASS?

BE UNABLE TO MOVE YOUR BODY EVERY TIME IT RAINS *or* NOT BE ABLE TO STOP MOVING WHILE THE SUN IS OUT?

BE THE FIRST PERSON TO EXPLORE A PLANET *or* BE THE INVENTOR OF A CURE FOR A DEADLY DISEASE?

HAVE UNLIMITED INTERNATIONAL FIRST-CLASS TICKETS *or* NEVER PAY FOR FOOD AT RESTAURANTS?

HAVE YOUR ONLY MODE OF TRANSPORTATION BE A DONKEY *or* AN ELEPHANT?

LIVE IN A CAVE *or* LIVE IN A TREE HOUSE?

NEVER BE ABLE TO LEAVE YOUR OWN COUNTRY *or* NEVER BE ABLE TO FLY IN A PLANE AGAIN?

ALWAYS FEEL LIKE SOMEONE IS FOLLOWING YOU *or* ALWAYS FEEL LIKE SOMEONE IS WATCHING YOU?

BE FLUENT IN ALL LANGUAGES AND NEVER ABLE TO TRAVEL *or* BE ABLE TO TRAVEL ANYWHERE BUT NEVER ABLE TO LEARN A DIFFERENT LANGUAGE?

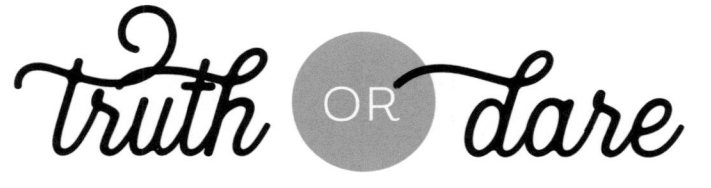

truth OR dare

Challenge yourself! Don't hold back!

TRUTH: What makes you feel most confident?

DARE: Make and wear a 'Free Hugs' sign around today.

TRUTH: What is one of your biggest regrets?

TRUTH: What are you most afraid will happen in your lifetime?

DARE: Spend an entire day alone.

TRUTH: What's the first thing you think of when you think of yourself?

TRUTH: What book has changed your life?

DARE: Leave little inspiring notes around for others to find.

TRUTH: How do you behave when you're angry?

DARE: Tell at least 5 people that you love them.

TRUTH: When are you the happiest?

TRUTH: What do you spend the most time thinking about?

TRUTH: What's one secret you've never told anyone?

DARE: Wear something "crazy" today. Something that, for you, is unexpected. Be daring!

TRUTH: What is the single most important thing in your world right now?

TRUTH: What's something you've done purely out of peer pressure?

DARE: Say 'Yes!' to everything today.

TRUTH: What things are you not likely to ask for help with?

DARE: Tell yourself only kind things today.

DARE: Compliment 10 strangers today.

TRUTH: What makes you feel most vulnerable?

DARE: Do something kind for someone but remain anonymous.

Write down your **NOMAD STORY**—your point of view on what it feels like when you're a nomad and a global explorer and an adventurer.

Write all of your thoughts and theories and feelings about what makes you a mighty first-rate nomad.

_____

_____

_____

_____

_____

_____

_____

_____

_____

_____

_____

_____

_____

_____

_____

_____

_____

_____

_____

As you travel through the world, you're bound to have brilliant realizations, crazy insights and sudden inspiration—if you're open to them. Here's where you can write these things down.

Record your aha moments and determine how they will help you continue moving, only forward!

DAREDEVIL

EPIC

Mighty
NOMAD
★★★★★★★
★

Go
GETTER

— *Rad* —
HUMAN

....*The*....
GOOD
— ENOUGHIST —
Society
★

Reckless
AND
BRAVE

....

CHAPTER FOUR

MIGHTY

ENTHUSIAST

MIGHTY
ENTHUSIAST

....

THIS CHAPTER CHAMPIONS
every brilliant observer, any curious
believers, all wild hopefuls and every
classification of top-notch enthusiast.
Find your voice here by gathering all
you can, rallying other aficionados,
soaking up anything and everything
around and being a ready and willing
student of every little thing.

Let's just say
YOU GOT THIS!

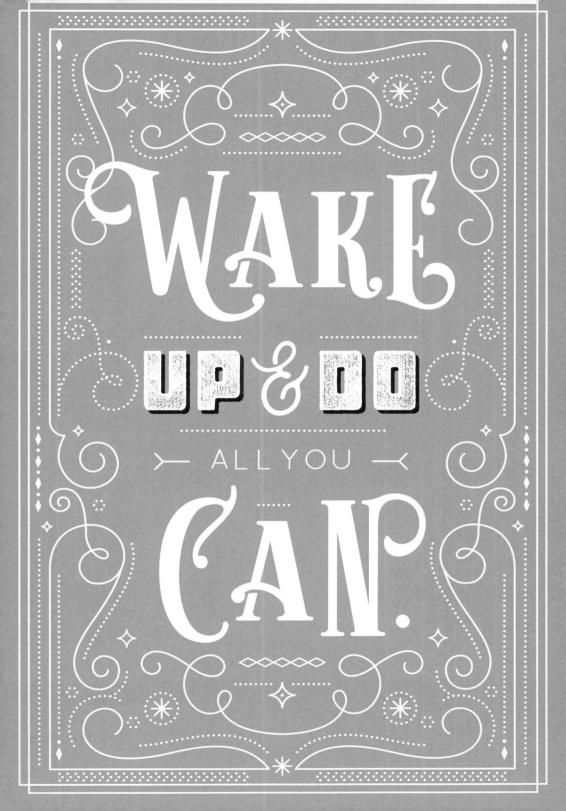

Two distinguished professors?

_____

_____

What makes them so decidedly distinguished?

_____

_____

_____

Two surprising specialists?

_____

_____

What makes them so decidedly surprising?

_____

_____

_____

Two superb mentors?

_____

_____

What makes them so decidedly superb?

_____

_____

_____

Two fascinating scholars?

_____

_____

What makes them so decidedly fascinating?

_____

_____

_____

Two awesome principals?

_____

_____

What makes them so decidedly awesome?

_____

_____

_____

Burning
QUESTIONS

Write, record, ruminate, chew over, cogitate and ponder *all* your burning questions about full-fledged enthusiasts, lifelong learning and shameless curiosity. What would you ask if you could ask absolutely anything?

Do one thing every day
THAT IS
CURIOUS

_____   _____

_____   _____

_____   _____

_____   _____

_____   _____

_____   _____

_____   _____

_____   _____

_____   _____

_____   _____

QUESTION Everything

What makes a learner a learner?

_____

_____

_____

What jobs interest you?

_____

_____

_____

What are the worst jobs you've ever heard of?

_____

_____

_____

When did you last try something new?

_____

_____

_____

If you could be the best in the world at something, what would it be?

_____

_____

_____

What's an embarrassing life goal you have?

_____

_____

_____

100 CURIOUS

Sketches

Take these two pages and pencil in, scribble about, trace and sketch the first 100 curious things you think of. The sheer number gets you through the obvious and on to the good stuff. Let's see what you uncover!

Don't stop now, keep sketching!

What

ARE YOU

GOING TO DO

— with all this —

FUTURE?

Curious SCAVENGER

· · · · · · · · · · · · · · · · · ·

Set out on a scavenger hunt!
Take pictures, collect things
& size up your findings!

☐ **LOCAL OR STREET MUSICIANS**
Date: Location:
Description:

☐ **SOMEONE READING A BOOK**
Date: Location:
Description:

☐ **A OLD SET OF ENCYCLOPEDIAS**
Date: Location:
Description:

☐ **A DOCTORAL DIPLOMA**
Date: Location:
Description:

☐ **A FANCY SIGNATURE**
Date: Location:
Description:

☐ **SOMETHING IN BRAILLE**
Date: Location:
Description:

☐ **AN UNEDITED STORY**
Date: Location:
Description:

☐ **A RARE BOOK**
Date: Location:
Description:

☐ **A RESEARCH LAB**
Date: Location:
Description:

☐ **A LOCAL LIBRARY CARD**
Date: Location:
Description:

Notes:

○ Donate your old books to your local library

○ Tutor someone younger than you

○ Create a list of all your favorite books and leave copies in bookstores for people to find

○ Locate every local library in your state or region

○ Leave 50 famous quotes in unexpected places

○ Build your own little free library

○ Visit 10 bookstores in one day

○ Take an IQ test (then, rip up the results)

○ Share your knowledge of technology with a senior citizen

○ Get a psychic reading

○ Write 10 important letters to your future self

○ Volunteer as an assistant to a teacher

○ Attend an annual library book sale

○ Create your own tutorial to post online

○ Write down 100 questions you have about anything

○ Research your own personal superhero

○ Read 50 books this year

○ Teach someone about your favorite topic

NOTES:

_____

_____

_____

_____

_____

_____

COMPOSE *Your* OWN

Compose, write, format, scheme and fashion your very own mighty book label ideas.
Find all the ways to be resolute, deliberate and bold with your mighty works.

BE A JOURNALIST

Be a journalist, a writer, a reporter and a storyteller!
Go out into your community, area and around your familiar
stomping grounds and start asking other humans bold and
interesting questions about how they are mighty enthusiasts
and believers in the world.

ASK 10 QUESTIONS:
(Be gutsy and bold with who you chat with. Ask the hard stuff. Ask it all.)

_____

_____

_____

_____

_____

_____

_____

_____

_____

_____

_____

_____

_____

_____

_____

_____

_____

_____

_____

NOTICE EVERY DETAIL:
(This is where you'll likely hear the *real* story, the good stuff and the whole truth.)

_____

_____

_____

_____

_____

_____

_____

_____

_____

_____

_____

_____

_____

_____

_____

_____

_____

_____

_____

_____

_____

_____

_____

_____

_____

Now, after you've collected your thoughts, their thoughts, all the brilliant
details and all points of view and notions, evaluate, digest and try to sum
up the new knowledge into your own mighty format (as a soap box orator,
a slam poet, a singer/songwriter or a political character).
Use your voice to report the findings.

FUTURE SELF *Letters*

Write things down to read later. Write about yourself—you as an individual and a good human. What will you have done? What will you have accomplished in this vast future of yours? What will you have seen, read, witnessed, experienced? This is where you change the game!

Dear _____ ,

_____

_____

_____

_____

_____

_____

Dear _____ ,

_____

_____

_____

_____

_____

_____

_____

Dear _____ ,

_____

_____

_____

_____

_____

_____

Dear _____ ,

_____

_____

_____

_____

_____

_____

Dear _____ ,

_____

_____

_____

_____

_____

_____

$\mathcal{My}$ COLLECTION

Over the course of a week, set a goal to collect, gather, round up and compile all things that make you feel like a real enthusiast! (Maybe a rare book, a vintage pen, an old report card or a famous person's résumé) Draw, identify and record them here.

ITEM: _____

_____

DATE: _____

ITEM: _____

_____

DATE: _____

ITEM: _____

_____

DATE: _____

ITEM: _____

_____

DATE: _____

ITEM: _____

_____

DATE: _____

ITEM: _____

_____

DATE: _____

ITEM: _____

_____

DATE: _____

ITEM: _____

_____

DATE: _____

ITEM:

_____

_____

DATE:

_____

ITEM:

_____

_____

DATE:

_____

ITEM:

_____

_____

DATE:

_____

ITEM:

_____

_____

DATE:

_____

ITEM:

_____

_____

DATE:

_____

ITEM:

_____

_____

DATE:

_____

ITEM:

_____

_____

DATE:

_____

ITEM:

_____

_____

DATE:

_____

ITEM:

_____

_____

DATE:

_____

ITEM:

_____

_____

DATE:

_____

Oh, ALL THE BOOKS I'LL READ!

Dig into the more meaningful things, every manner of significance, and, most especially, your far-reaching future. Explore and record all of the brilliant literature you'd like to read. I'm guessing you'll surprise yourself with one mighty list!

_____   _____

_____   _____

_____   _____

_____   _____

_____   _____

_____   _____

_____   _____

_____   _____

_____   _____

_____   _____

_____   _____

_____   _____

Would you RATHER?

(circle your answers)

KNOW ALL THE MYSTERIES OF THE UNIVERSE *or* KNOW EVERY OUTCOME OF EVERY CHOICE YOU MAKE?

NEVER HEAR MUSIC AGAIN *or* LOSE THE ABILITY TO READ?

BE ABLE TO SPEAK WHALE *or* READ BABIES' MINDS?

HAVE A HIGHER IQ *or* A PHOTOGRAPHIC MEMORY?

LOSE THE ABILITY TO HEAR *or* LOSE THE ABILITY TO SPEAK?

HAVE A HORRIBLE SHORT-TERM MEMORY *or* A HORRIBLE LONG-TERM MEMORY?

LOSE THE ABILITY TO READ *or* THE ABILITY TO SING?

HAVE ONE REAL GET-OUT-OF-JAIL-FREE CARD *or* A KEY THAT OPENS ANY DOOR?

BRUSH YOUR TEETH WITH HOT SAUCE *or* BRUSH YOUR TEETH WITH RANCH DRESSING?

BE COMPLETELY INSANE AND KNOW THAT YOU ARE INSANE *or* COMPLETELY INSANE AND BELIEVE YOU ARE SANE?

BE A PRACTICING DOCTOR *or* A MEDICAL RESEARCHER?

HAVE LEGS AS LONG AS YOUR FINGERS *or* HAVE FINGERS AS LONG AS YOUR LEGS?

FORCED TO EAT ONLY SPICY FOOD *or* TO EAT ONLY INCREDIBLY BLAND FOOD?

BE AMAZINGLY FAST AT TYPING *or* BE ABLE TO READ RIDICULOUSLY FAST?

NEVER HAVE TO WORK AGAIN *or* NEVER HAVE TO SLEEP AGAIN?

HAVE YOUR DREAM JOB *or* ONE THAT PAYS FOUR TIMES AS MUCH?

ALWAYS BE ABLE TO SEE 5 MINUTES INTO THE FUTURE *or* 100 YEARS INTO THE FUTURE?

Letter WRITER'S REVIVAL

Bring back letter writing! Write a letter, a pile of postcards or tons of lengthy correspondences to **genius scholars who have changed your thinking**. Ask questions, be curious, be bold, be genuine, be real, be interested. Write right now!

LETTER TO:

_____

QUESTIONS TO ASK:

_____
_____
_____

LETTER TO:

_____

QUESTIONS TO ASK:

_____
_____
_____

LETTER TO:

_____

QUESTIONS TO ASK:

_____
_____
_____

WHAT'S *Your* STORY?

Write down your **ENTHUSIAST STORY**—your point of view on what it feels like when you're an enthusiast and a thinker and an observer.

Write all of your thoughts and theories and feelings about what makes you a mighty first-rate enthusiast.

_____

_____

_____

_____

_____

_____

_____

_____

_____

_____

_____

_____

_____

_____

_____

_____

_____

_____

_____

_____

_____

AHA!

As you travel through the world, you're bound to have brilliant realizations, crazy insights and sudden inspiration—if you're open to them. Here's where you can write these things down.

Record your aha moments and determine how they will help you continue moving, only forward!

Mighty **BADGES**

YOU'VE
EARNED
YOUR
STRIPES

TOTALCHAMP

····· ☆ ·····
SHINING
STAR

GOLDEN

★
RADNESS
—Society—

★
Mighty
ENTHU
SIAST
·········
···

Mighty
—UP—
AND
COMER

····· The ·····
BONA FIDE
····· Best ·····

CHAPTER FIVE

MIGHTY SIDEKICK

MIGHTY SIDEKICK

....

THIS CHAPTER CHAMPIONS

ever gutsy accomplice, all forthright
comrades, any awesome chum
and every order of mighty sidekick.
Find your voice here by building
bold relationships, joining in on
worthwhile exchanges, working on
wise communication and deciding
your intrinsic place in all of it.

Well,

READY FREDDIE?

NO ONE

has ever made

— THEMSELF —

GREAT

— by showing —

— HOW —

SMALL

someone else

IS.

Can you NAME:

Two far-reaching community leaders?

_____

_____

What makes them so decidedly far-reaching?

_____

_____

_____

Two relevant public relations specialists?

_____

_____

What makes them so decidedly relevant?

_____

_____

_____

Two foremost psychologists?

_____

_____

What makes them so decidedly foremost?

_____

_____

_____

Two effective volunteers?

_____

_____

What makes them so decidedly effective?

_____

_____

_____

Two meaningful event planners?

_____

_____

What makes them so decidedly meaningful?

_____

_____

_____

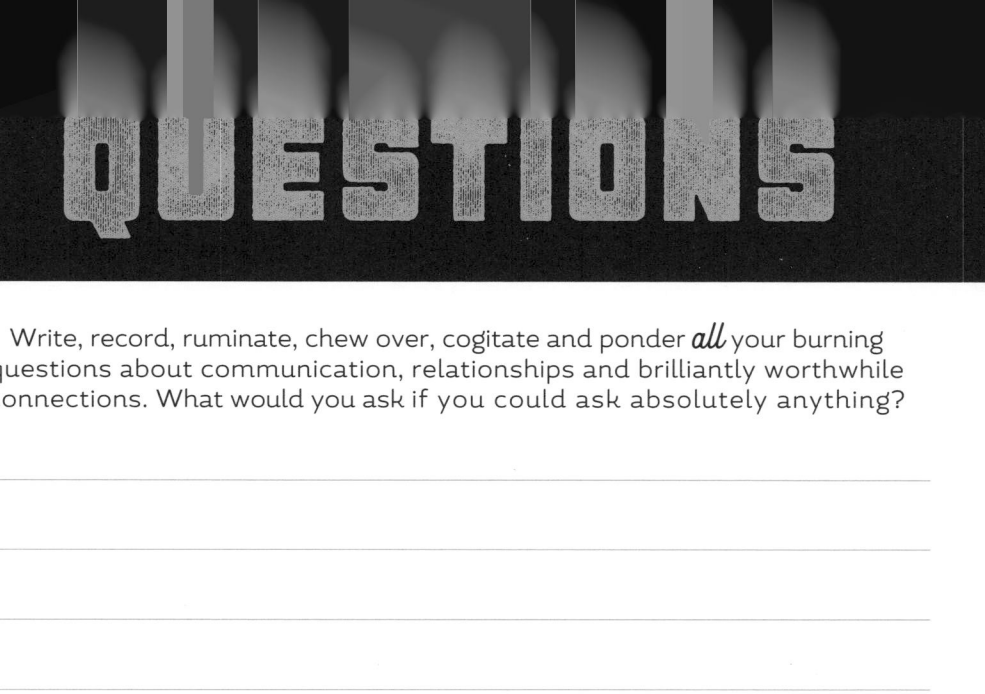

QUESTIONS

Write, record, ruminate, chew over, cogitate and ponder *all* your burning questions about communication, relationships and brilliantly worthwhile connections. What would you ask if you could ask absolutely anything?

Do one thing every day
THAT IS
NEIGHBORLY

_____ _____

_____ _____

_____ _____

_____ _____

_____ _____

_____ _____

_____ _____

_____ _____

_____ _____

_____ _____

_____ _____

QUESTION Everything

What makes a friend a friend?

_____

_____

_____

Who is your hero?

_____

_____

_____

Who in the world would you like to meet?

_____

_____

_____

What is something someone told you that wasn't true?

_____

_____

_____

If people could see inside you, what would they see?

_____

_____

_____

If you could build a family out of your friends, who would you include?

_____

_____

_____

100 FRIENDLY *Sketches*

Take these two pages and pencil in, scribble about, trace and sketch the first 100 friendly things you think of. The sheer number gets you through the obvious and on to the good stuff. Let's see what you uncover!

Don't stop now, keep sketching!

DO

SMALL

things

— WITH GREAT —

LOVE.

Friendly
SCAVENGER

· · · · · · · · · · · · · · · · ·

Set out on a scavenger hunt!
Take pictures, collect things
& size up your findings!

☐ **LYRICS TO A LOVE SONG**

Date: Location:

Description: _____

_____

_____

☐ **A STRANGER'S AUTOGRAPH**

Date: Location:

Description: _____

_____

_____

☐ **A VINTAGE FAMILY PHOTO**

Date: Location:

Description: _____

_____

_____

☐ **AN OLD PHOTOGRAPH**

Date: Location:

Description: _____

_____

_____

☐ **A LETTER FROM A PEN PAL**

Date: Location:

Description: _____

_____

_____

☐ **SOMEONE SHAKING HANDS**

Date: Location:

Description: _____

_____

_____

☐ **THE WORD "FRIEND"**

Date: Location:

Description: _____

_____

_____

☐ **SOMETHING WITH THE WORD "WELCOME"**

Date: Location:

Description: _____

_____

_____

☐ **SOMETHING HEART-SHAPED**

Date: Location:

Description: _____

_____

_____

☐ **A BFF NECKLACE**

Date: Location:

Description: _____

_____

_____

Notes:

_____

_____

_____

_____

- ○ Volunteer at a food pantry
- ○ Locate every religious organization in your city
- ○ Introduce yourself to ALL your neighbors
- ○ Organize a community yard sale
- ○ Play in a park with the kids!
- ○ Write a story about your most interesting friend
- ○ Volunteer at a town hall meeting or community event
- ○ Say hello to EVERYONE you pass today
- ○ Volunteer with senior citizens
- ○ Learn some family history
- ○ Chalk draw hopscotch drawings around your local park
- ○ Run a community bake sale
- ○ Identify the top 10 reasons for being a mighty volunteer
- ○ Plan and execute a community water balloon fight
- ○ Go and swing on some swings
- ○ Foster a rescue pet
- ○ Give strangers high fives for a day
- ○ Draw your own family tree
- ○ Write 30 snail mail letters in 30 days

NOTES:

_____

_____

_____

_____

_____

PLAN *Your* OWN

Plan, write, pen, ink, generate, and hatch your very own thank-you note ideas. Lean into your kindness and use your heart to help these show some soul!

BE A JOURNALIST

Be a journalist, a writer, a reporter and a storyteller!
Go out into your community, area and around your familiar
stomping grounds and start asking other humans bold and
interesting questions about how they are mighty accomplices
and comrades in the world.

ASK 10 QUESTIONS:
(Be gutsy and bold with who you chat with. Ask the hard stuff. Ask it all.)

_____

_____

_____

_____

_____

_____

_____

_____

_____

_____

_____

_____

_____

_____

_____

_____

_____

_____

_____

_____

_____

_____

NOTICE EVERY DETAIL:

(This is where you'll likely hear the *real* story, the good stuff and the whole truth.)

_____
_____
_____
_____
_____
_____
_____
_____
_____
_____
_____
_____
_____
_____
_____
_____
_____
_____
_____
_____
_____
_____
_____

Now, after you've collected your thoughts, their thoughts, all the brilliant details and all points of view and notions, evaluate, digest and try to sum up the new knowledge into your own mighty format (as a soap box orator, a slam poet, a singer/songwriter or a political character).
Use your voice to report the findings.

BUILD YOUR *Own*

Create your own support system for your life. Surround yourself with only the good and only those you choose to let in. Who are these people? What are their roles? What importance do they have to you? (These could be people you've known your entire life, people you've not yet met in real life, friends who live across the country or world, someone in your same city, familiar faces you'd like to get to know and maybe even a complete stranger or two...you decide.)

Person

_____

Role

_____

Importance

_____

_____

_____

Person

_____

Role

_____

Importance

_____

_____

_____

Person

_____

Role

_____

Importance

_____

_____

_____

Person

_____

Role

_____

Importance

_____

_____

_____

Person

_____

Role

_____

Importance

_____

_____

_____

Person

_____

Role

_____

Importance

_____

_____

_____

WRITER'S REVIVAL

Bring back letter writing! Write a letter, a pile of postcards or tons of lengthy correspondences to **prospective pen pals you've always wanted to know**. Ask questions, be curious, be bold, be genuine, be real, be interested. Write right now!

LETTER TO:

_____

QUESTIONS TO ASK:

_____

_____

_____

LETTER TO:

_____

QUESTIONS TO ASK:

_____

_____

_____

LETTER TO:

_____

QUESTIONS TO ASK:

_____

_____

_____

YOUR INNER *Socialist*

Today, do some people watching. They might just be someone in a crowd, a random passerby, a not-so-innocent bystander. Notice things, notice humanity, notice your reactions and thoughts. Just notice. Then write your observations.

○ AN UNLIKELY HERO
○ AN OVERWORKED CEO
○ AN ASPIRING REBEL
○ A SLOW-TO-START ADVENTURER
○ _____

AGE:

WHAT ARE THEY THINKING ABOUT RIGHT NOW?
_____
_____
_____

WHAT KIND OF SECRETS DO THEY HAVE?
_____
_____
_____

○ AN UNLIKELY HERO
○ AN OVERWORKED CEO
○ AN ASPIRING REBEL
○ A SLOW-TO-START ADVENTURER
○ _____

AGE:

WHAT ARE THEY THINKING ABOUT RIGHT NOW?
_____
_____
_____

WHAT KIND OF SECRETS DO THEY HAVE?
_____
_____
_____

○ AN UNLIKELY HERO
○ AN OVERWORKED CEO
○ AN ASPIRING REBEL
○ A SLOW-TO-START ADVENTURER
○ _____

AGE:

WHAT ARE THEY THINKING ABOUT RIGHT NOW?
_____
_____
_____

WHAT KIND OF SECRETS DO THEY HAVE?
_____
_____

○ AN UNLIKELY HERO
○ AN OVERWORKED CEO
○ AN ASPIRING REBEL
○ A SLOW-TO-START ADVENTURER
○ _____

AGE:

WHAT ARE THEY THINKING ABOUT RIGHT NOW?
_____
_____
_____

WHAT KIND OF SECRETS DO THEY HAVE?
_____
_____

○ AN UNLIKELY HERO
○ AN OVERWORKED CEO
○ AN ASPIRING REBEL
○ A SLOW-TO-START ADVENTURER
○ _____

AGE:

WHAT ARE THEY THINKING ABOUT RIGHT NOW?

_____

_____

_____

WHAT KIND OF SECRETS DO THEY HAVE?

_____

_____

_____

○ AN UNLIKELY HERO
○ AN OVERWORKED CEO
○ AN ASPIRING REBEL
○ A SLOW-TO-START ADVENTURER
○ _____

AGE:

WHAT ARE THEY THINKING ABOUT RIGHT NOW?

_____

_____

_____

WHAT KIND OF SECRETS DO THEY HAVE?

_____

_____

_____

○ AN UNLIKELY HERO
○ AN OVERWORKED CEO
○ AN ASPIRING REBEL
○ A SLOW-TO-START ADVENTURER
○ _____

AGE:

WHAT ARE THEY THINKING ABOUT RIGHT NOW?

_____

_____

_____

WHAT KIND OF SECRETS DO THEY HAVE?

_____

_____

_____

○ AN UNLIKELY HERO
○ AN OVERWORKED CEO
○ AN ASPIRING REBEL
○ A SLOW-TO-START ADVENTURER
○ _____

AGE:

WHAT ARE THEY THINKING ABOUT RIGHT NOW?

_____

_____

_____

WHAT KIND OF SECRETS DO THEY HAVE?

_____

_____

_____

NOTES:

_____

_____

_____

_____

_____

  PEOPLE I'LL MEET!

Dig into the more meaningful things, every manner of significance, and, most especially, your far-reaching future. Look for and record all of the brilliant humans you meet and love. I'm guessing you'll surprise yourself with one mighty list!

Would you RATHER?

(circle your answers)

BE HELD IN HIGH REGARD BY YOUR COMMUNITY *or* THE MEDIA?

RATHER HAVE SOMEONE DO EVERYTHING FOR YOU *or* DO IT YOURSELF?

MOVE TO A NEW CITY OR TOWN EVERY WEEK *or* NEVER BE ABLE TO LEAVE THE CITY OR TOWN YOU WERE BORN IN?

FORCED TO DANCE EVERY TIME YOU HEARD MUSIC *or* FORCED TO SING ANY SONG YOU HEARD?

HAVE TOO MANY FRIENDS *or* HAVE TOO FEW?

WEAR WEDDING ATTIRE EVERY SINGLE DAY *or* A BATHING SUIT EVERY SINGLE DAY?

NEVER BE ABLE TO EAT MEAT *or* NEVER BE ABLE TO EAT VEGETABLES?

LOSE YOUR BEST FRIEND *or* LOSE ALL OF YOUR FRIENDS EXCEPT FOR YOUR BEST FRIEND?

LOSE ALL YOUR MONEY AND VALUABLES *or* LOSE ALL THE PICTURES YOU HAVE EVER TAKEN?

BE FEARED BY ALL *or* LOVED BY ALL?

NEVER GET ANGRY *or* NEVER BE ENVIOUS?

BE INCREDIBLY POOR BUT HELP PEOPLE *or* BECOME INCREDIBLY RICH BY HURTING PEOPLE?

SNITCH ON YOUR BEST FRIEND FOR A CRIME *or* GO TO JAIL FOR YOUR BEST FRIEND'S CRIME?

HAVE YOU *Ever*

- ○ Had a pen pal
- ○ Distributed secret messages
- ○ Talked to a stranger
- ○ Paid for someone else's meal
- ○ Been president of something
- ○ Just smiled for an entire day
- ○ Thrown a dinner party for friends
- ○ Written fan mail
- ○ Done extensive people watching
- ○ Chatted with a bus driver
- ○ Interviewed a psychologist
- ○ Given someone a tour of your city
- ○ Taken a stranger to lunch
- ○ Called up a long-lost friend
- ○ Played on a playground alone

- ○ Attended a town meeting
- ○ Said yes to everything
- ○ Written to your hero
- ○ Revealed a secret
- ○ Made chalk drawings on the sidewalk
- ○ Played 20 Questions
- ○ Volunteered at a shelter
- ○ Paid for the person behind you in line
- ○ Written a snail mail letter
- ○ Told your story
- ○ Taken groceries in for your neighbor
- ○ Planned a picnic
- ○ Given a rave review
- ○ Said hi to 50 strangers in one day
- ○ Told your friends you love them

Give yourself points if you want to: _____

WHAT'S *Your* STORY?

Write down your **SIDEKICK STORY**—your point of view on what it feels like when you're a sidekick and an accomplice and an awesome chum.

Write all of your thoughts and theories and feelings about what makes you a mighty first-rate sidekick.

_____

_____

_____

_____

_____

_____

_____

_____

_____

_____

_____

_____

_____

_____

_____

_____

_____

_____

_____

AHA!

As you travel through the world, you're bound to have brilliant realizations, crazy insights and sudden inspiration—if you're open to them. Here's where you can write these things down.

Record your aha moments and determine how they will help you continue moving, only forward!

Mighty **BADGES** YOU'VE EARNED YOUR STRIPES

GOODHUMAN

Mighty CHAMP IONER

★★★ Mighty ★★★ SIDEKICK

- SUPER - DUPER

Gosh DANG PHENOMENAL

WELL MANNERED Pacifist

High FIVE - CLUB -

CHAPTER SIX

....

MUSE

MIGHTY
MUSE

....

THIS CHAPTER CHAMPIONS
every novel creator, any ungoverned
artist, all nonsensical thinkers and
every style of fearless dreamer. Find
your voice here by doing all you can
to be you, seeking out all the
brilliantly uncommon, encouraging
only the one of a kind and doing
the unprecedented in everything.

Go on Now,

BANG YOUR OWN DRUM!

I'M **GOING** TO MAKE *EVERYTHING* around me BEAUTIFUL — THAT WILL BE — my — LIFE.

ELSIE DE WOLFE

Can you NAME:

Two celebrated artists?

_____

_____

What makes them so decidedly celebrated?

_____

_____

_____

Two ace inventors?

_____

_____

What makes them so decidedly ace?

_____

_____

_____

Two masterful writers?

_____

_____

What makes them so decidedly masterful?

_____

_____

_____

Two illustrious makers?

_____

_____

What makes them so decidedly illustrious?

_____

_____

_____

Two reputable thinkers?

_____

_____

What makes them so decidedly reputable?

_____

_____

_____

Burning

QUESTIONS

Write, record, ruminate, chew over, cogitate and ponder *all* your burning
questions about creativity, daydreaming and clever introspection.
What would you ask if you could ask absolutely anything?

Do one thing every day
THAT IS
CREATIVE

_____   _____

_____   _____

_____   _____

_____   _____

_____   _____

_____   _____

_____   _____

_____   _____

_____   _____

_____   _____

_____   _____

QUESTION *Everything*

What makes a creator a creator?

_____

_____

_____

What do you daydream about?

_____

_____

_____

What is your most frequent singular thought?

_____

_____

_____

What is the best part of you?

_____

_____

_____

What kinds of things do you like to stockpile?

_____

_____

_____

What one important thing would you like to create?

_____

_____

_____

100 RARE
Sketches

Take these two pages and pencil in, scribble about, trace
and sketch the first 100 rare things you think of. The sheer
number gets you through the obvious and on to the good stuff.
Let's see what you uncover!

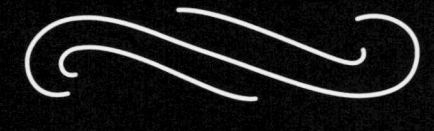

Ordinary

LIFE

DOES NOT

INTEREST

me.

ANAÏS NIN

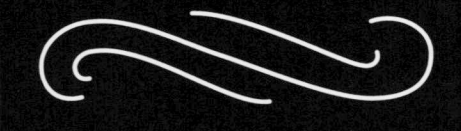

Creative
SCAVENGER

· · · · · · · · · · · · · · · · · ·

Set out on a scavenger hunt!
Take pictures, collect things
& size up your findings!

☐ A SIDEWALK CHALK DRAWING
Date: Location:

Description:
_____
_____
_____

☐ A SELF-PORTRAIT
Date: Location:

Description:
_____
_____
_____

☐ THE FUNNIEST THING YOU CAN FIND
Date: Location:

Description:
_____
_____
_____

☐ A VINTAGE WRITING TOOL
Date: Location:

Description:
_____
_____
_____

☐ A LOCAL ART GALLERY
Date: Location:

Description:
_____
_____
_____

☐ AN ANIMAL SHAPE IN THE CLOUDS
Date: Location:

Description:
_____
_____
_____

☐ GRAFFITI ART
Date: Location:

Description:
_____
_____
_____

☐ A COLLECTION
Date: Location:

Description:
_____
_____
_____

☐ A FLYER FOR AN ART SHOW
Date: Location:

Description:
_____
_____
_____

☐ THE WORD "CURIOUS"
Date: Location:

Description:
_____
_____
_____

Notes:
_____
_____
_____
_____

- ○ Create a public art piece
- ○ Meet up with a group of creatives for breakfast
- ○ Sell your creative wares at a local market
- ○ Create a community mural
- ○ Take 50 photos of just color in one week
- ○ Lie on the grass and identify 20 cloud animals
- ○ Take 30 self portraits in 30 days
- ○ Draw 30 self portraits in 30 days
- ○ Help promote a local art gallery or show
- ○ Make your very first zine
- ○ Learn an antiquated printing technique
- ○ Invent a new (to you) art technique
- ○ Rewrite history in a journal
- ○ Make chalk graffiti art throughout your town
- ○ Try a new musical instrument
- ○ Volunteer at an art camp for kids
- ○ Take photos of rad typography
- ○ Take on a new artistic hobby
- ○ Volunteer your time in a public school art class
- ○ Get extra messy!
- ○ Design and print your own daring stickers
- ○ Donate your artwork to a silent auction
- ○ Keep a drawing journal of all things important to you
- ○ Photograph your feet in every place you enter for one week
- ○ Start a collection of something rare

DESIGN *Your* OWN

Design, hand letter, illustrate, draw, create, paint, color your very own mighty badges. Use your own voice, your favorite phrases, some rad idioms, witty concepts and brilliant sayings to make them especially mighty.

BE A JOURNALIST

Be a journalist, a writer, a reporter and a storyteller!
Go out into your community, area and around your familiar
stomping grounds and start asking other humans bold and
interesting questions about how they are mighty artists and
creators in the world.

ASK 10 QUESTIONS:
(Be gutsy and bold with who you chat with. Ask the hard stuff. Ask it all.)

NOTICE EVERY DETAIL:

(This is where you'll likely hear the *real* story, the good stuff and the whole truth.)

_____

_____

_____

_____

_____

_____

_____

_____

_____

_____

_____

_____

_____

_____

_____

_____

_____

_____

_____

_____

_____

_____

_____

_____

Now, after you've collected your thoughts, their thoughts, all the brilliant
details and all points of view and notions, evaluate, digest and try to sum
up the new knowledge into your own mighty format (as a soap box orator,
a slam poet, a singer/songwriter or a political character).
Use your voice to report the findings.

WHO ARE YOU?

Take a photo of yourself every day for seven days.
Use the same framing, location or background and time of day
for every photo. Write down all your creative discoveries.

DAY 1: _____

_____

_____

DAY 2: _____

_____

_____

DAY 3: _____

_____

_____

DAY 4: _____

_____

_____

DAY 5: _____

_____

_____

DAY 6: _____

_____

_____

DAY 7: _____

_____

_____

WRITER'S REVIVAL

Bring back letter writing! Write a letter, a pile of postcards or tons of lengthy correspondences to **celebrated artists who are mighty creatives**. Ask questions, be curious, be bold, be genuine, be real, be interested. Write right now!

LETTER TO:

_____

QUESTIONS TO ASK:

_____
_____
_____

LETTER TO:

_____

QUESTIONS TO ASK:

_____
_____
_____

LETTER TO:

_____

QUESTIONS TO ASK:

_____
_____
_____

SMALL & MIGHTY

What are the small things that make you happy? Draw all of those things. Maybe you'll discover that a page full of seemingly insignificant things can turn into something mighty.

TITLE:

TITLE:

TITLE:

TITLE:

TITLE:

TITLE:

TITLE:

TITLE:

TITLE:

TITLE:

TITLE:

TITLE:

TITLE:

TITLE:

TITLE:

TITLE:

TITLE:

TITLE:

TITLE:

TITLE:

TITLE:

TITLE:

TITLE:

TITLE:

TITLE:

TITLE:

TITLE:

DRAW *Your* SELFIE

Draw a self-portrait, a sketch, a likeness, or depiction of yourself below. Draw a few, draw several, create a variety of styles or change your own appearance. Who do you see and what do you love about them?!

Would you RATHER?

(circle your answers)

WEAR CLOWN SHOES EVERY DAY *or* WEAR A CLOWN WIG EVERY DAY?

CREATE A GREAT PIECE OF ART AND NOT GET CREDIT *or* GET CREDIT FOR A PIECE OF ART YOU DIDN'T CREATE?

BECOME A CREATIVE PERSON *or* A TECHNICAL PERSON?

TRY SOMETHING NEW *or* STICK TO WHAT YOU KNOW?

HAVE EVERYTHING YOU DRAW BECOME REAL BUT BE PERMANENTLY TERRIBLE AT DRAWING *or* BE ABLE TO FLY BUT ONLY AS FAST AS YOU CAN WALK?

HAVE AN EASY JOB WORKING FOR SOMEONE ELSE *or* WORK FOR YOURSELF BUT WORK INCREDIBLY HARD?

GO BACK TO AGE 5 WITH EVERYTHING YOU KNOW NOW *or* KNOW NOW EVERYTHING YOUR FUTURE SELF WILL LEARN?

ONLY WEAR ONE COLOR EACH DAY *or* HAVE TO WEAR SEVEN COLORS EACH DAY?

BE A FAMOUS DIRECTOR *or* BE A FAMOUS ACTOR?

HAVE NO TASTE BUDS *or* BE COLOR BLIND?

EAT A DRY BOX OF SPAGHETTI *or* EAT TWO CUPS OF UNCOOKED RICE?

BORN AGAIN IN A TOTALLY DIFFERENT LIFE *or* BORN AGAIN WITH ALL THE KNOWLEDGE YOU HAVE NOW?

NOT BE ABLE TO SEE ANY COLORS *or* HAVE MILD BUT CONSTANT RINGING IN YOUR EARS?

BE AN AMAZING ARTIST BUT NOT BE ABLE TO SEE ANY OF THE ART YOU CREATED *or* BE AN AMAZING MUSICIAN BUT NOT BE ABLE TO HEAR ANY OF THE MUSIC YOU CREATE?

  THINGS
I'LL
MAKE!

Dig into the more meaningful things, every manner of significance, and, most especially, your far-reaching future. Decide and record all of the clever things you want to create. I'm guessing you'll surprise yourself with one mighty list!

_____

_____

WHAT'S *Your* STORY?

Write down your **MUSE STORY**—your point of view on what it feels like when you're a muse and a creator and a nonsensical thinker.

Write all of your thoughts and theories and feelings about what makes you a mighty first-rate muse.

_____

_____

_____

_____

_____

_____

_____

_____

_____

_____

_____

_____

_____

_____

_____

_____

_____

_____

_____

_____

_____

EPILOGUE

a sort of post script

DECIDE 50 THINGS

YOU WANT TO DO THIS YEAR:

THINGS to REMEMBER

SIGNIFICANT QUOTES, KIND COMPLIMENTS, WORDS OF WISDOM:

RAISE HELL, KID

MIGHTY NOTES
JOTTINGS & MUSINGS

TO ALL THOSE WHO HAVE
ONLY EVER FELT SMALL.
BE SMALL NO LONGER.

....

Design & Illustrations by

NICOLE LARUE

First Edition
24 23 22 21 20 5 4 3 2 1
Text © 2020 Nicole LaRue

Published by Gibbs Smith
P.O. Box 667 Layton, Utah 84041
1.800.835.4993 orders www.gibbs-smith.com
Designed by Nicole LaRue

PRINTED & BOUND IN CHINA

Gibbs Smith books are printed on either recycled, 100% post-consumer waste, FSC-certified papers or on paper produced from sustainable PEFC-certified forest/controlled wood source. Learn more at www.pefc.org.

ISBN: 978-1-4236-5411-7